Liquid State
Copyright © 2021 by Riley Webster

tellwell

Tellwell Talent
www.tellwell.ca

ISBN
978-0-2288-6249-9 (Paperback)

liquid state

by riley webster

To the women who came before me
Who did the best they could with what they knew
Who stood on their own two feet before carrying the weight of
another
Who showed me how to be strong
Thank you.

I'm fascinated by water.

Scrolling through photos on my phone you'll come across images of the ocean, puddles, lakes, rivers. No context, though. Just water. More and more water.

In some of the pictures I see my reflection, in others I see the sky, clouds, a bird flying overhead. My favourites are the ones where you can see what's underneath the ripples; looking deeper, past the colour of the reflection and underneath the surface, sometimes what's below surprises you.

In March 2020, the beginning of the pandemic lockdown, I was taking a daily plunge in the sea. At the time, this practice anchored me. Every day, I would go to the shore, drop my towel, and sprint into the water, letting out a scream as I did so. I'd emerge anew; alive, unguarded, ready.

In so much of the wording in these poems I speak about water. The element I connect with most as a Vancouver Island born and raised baby, water feels like home. It's adaptable, fluid. Here on the Island, water is held by mountains and islands; bays and rocky beaches. It takes the shape of whatever container it's in. When I embody water, I can travel to the depths of myself; the depths of everything. Whether it's calm and glasslike, stormy and chaotic, or something in-between, water is my mirror -- my constant reminder that nothing stays the same. That the ground beneath me is always moving.

I hope this collection of words and art helps you learn to be fluid with change and come home to yourself. I hope it reminds you that you're not alone. And I hope it helps you feel like letting go doesn't mean you're falling apart; rather, when you let yourself be liquid, you become open to whatever new form you take.

We cannot reach, grip, or grasp water; the only way to experience it is to be fully immersed.

xo Riley

I am not the message
I am a messenger
These words are not mine
They are Her's

And she's asking that we come home.

Within these pages is a whispering
A nudging
A gentle asking that you remember
You hold the earth
Wind
Air
Fire
Cosmos
Universe
In every cell
Breath
Piece of your wholeness.

I'd prefer to tell you something through poetry
The scrawl of the ink from my pen and the hasty fold in the
paper in which I write
The ease of each word that is part of my language but seems
to speak a new tongue
In letters that dance on my page, forming meaning.

I'd prefer to tell you something with my body
A soft sway in my low back and deep groove between my
upper thigh and hip as I sit in the last of the light
Wet hair cascading down my back, drying slowly in the
afternoon sun
The green in my eye glimmering when the rays reach my face
and I turn my chin up to the sky, asking for more.

I'd prefer to tell you something in energy
An unguarded heart apprehensively waiting for love to be
mirrored back
A deep gaze that looks past your wounds and to that clear
place where nothing has been touched
In openness, with backbone.

I'd prefer to tell you something on the eve of summer solstice
When the moon is high on a late-night sundown
When the air is thick with summer and anything feels
possible
When uncertainty feels like magic
Like mystery
Like a story waiting to be written.

The ocean's waves will always become still again
There's a rhythm to her when I let myself drift

I tune into the soft lapping of the shoreline and
My arms widen
My palms open
My body uncurls as my spine is once again held by the lulling
of the tide.

Rest.

I make it through the chaos when I remember that stillness is
always just moments away.

When you drop the need to be right
When you soften your edges, yet stand tall in your spine
When you understand the ways in which you try to maintain
control, and loosen your grip
When letting go of control feels impossible, yet you do it
anyway

Step by step

When you hear your calling, and begin to listen
When you understand that the melanin in your skin has
afforded you greater or lesser than the person sitting beside
you
When you're familiar with the indigenous territory upon
which you stand and offer thanks

Again and again

When you see your wounds without fixing
Covering
Shaming
But healing, because your inner work ripples into past
generations
Untangling the line of trauma that came before you
That is of you
That will not be passed down to your kids and their kids and
theirs once more

When you prioritize the collective over the individual
And equally allow pleasure over hustle
When you hear the soft echo of a bird above, the trickling
river, a car passing by and remember that you will never be
alone

When you surrender to the fact that the world is changing
When you're willing to start anew
When you're okay with being wrong
And wrong again
When you start a revolution through your authenticity
When you remember that joy is your birthright

Welcome to your liquid state.

I had to live in a cabin by the sea
No neighbours, only the lulling of the tide
I had to move away
Leave people behind
Rid myself of the information incoming
Never-ending
Inundating
So that I could hear my words again
So that I could birth my creations
So that I could remember who I am.

The container that held you has likely been stripped away. Watery in nature, you seek to find a new one. A career, an identity, a persona, a place, a relationship -- things outside of yourself that may hold you, if only for a short while. Containers are necessary, we can't always be liquid. But there are times for building and times for shedding. My gut tells me right now is for the latter. Unlearning, unbecoming, willing to begin again.

I've built walls around feeling to move through the world at the
pace I've been asked to keep up with. It's taken me years to go
back to pen and paper because I thought everything was about
speed. That's our training, right? Be rigid, tight, right, quick.
These walls have slowly started crumbling -- first inch by inch but
now they lie in rubble at my feet along with everything else that
wants to let go. An unraveling because I'm tired of carrying what
isn't mine. Ideas of who I should be, what I should do, how I'm
supposed to produce. When I get moments of stillness -- of space
between each stream of thought -- I remember: Soft bravery.
Gentle strength. Intuitive knowing. Fire on my tongue and
movement in my hips. Power that's grounded in earth and liquid
in state. Floating downstream, breath by breath, a river that moves
along as my heart races to catch up to the intelligence of Her.

To access my creativity, I need blank space.

Time alone. Time in nature. Time spent staring up at the clouds and watching them dance and transform. Time spent turning off so I can access what's underneath all the noise.

Quiet.

To access my well of ideas I gift myself the opportunity that lies in blank space. Unscheduled weekends and times of nothingness. Periods of not knowing. Of embracing uncertainty. Of letting what wants to be birthed be nourished, cared for, and connected to. Of stepping into the vulnerability that is creation.

I often fall into the tempting trap that is too much busyness. Until I access silence again. Until I create room for what wants to express through me. Until I receive what's available in this moment.

Opportunity waits for you in blank space.

Some blank space.

Are you breathing?

I go to the trees because I feel at home under their branches
Their soft soil at the base of their trunk a soft place for me to
land
I close my eyes and allow the vibration of the forest's
aliveness sync up with my own
Without effort
The stickiness and heaviness that has found my field melts
off me
I give it to the forest floor and she regenerates it
Cleansing the old so that I can welcome the new;
The new that is connected with the whole
I breathe out what's weighty and she transforms this breath
into her own
Sink sink sink
Even in the mud I don't skip her nutrients
I rest there and bathe in the heavy
In the dark
Because when I wash off the earth
Under my nails and in between my fingers
We are made of the same.

It's in this softness
Weightiness
Stillness
That the waves inside of you can flow
The tides of your own waters can lap your internal shoreline
The currents of your creativity
Your cycle
Your inklings
Have space to breathe again.

Receive
And receive some more.

The trick is
To let go of what doesn't
quite fit
So there's space
To dream again.

My gaze turns to the moon. I marvel at her always-changing nature, and reflect on how she glows each night. She shows up high in the night sky, no matter what's going on in the world that day. She doesn't cower when she's waxing or waning, nor does she boast in her fullness. She says, 'here I am, I may not be whole tonight, but love me just the same.' Consistently inconsistent, I see myself and all beings in her quiet illumination.

Pulled by the waters of her changing tides, when I flow with her seasons and rhythms I feel most at home.

Soul profiles. Energy readings. Human design. Astrology. Schools of thought that can give us information, but not answers. Remember your discernment -- remember what is real for you in your bones. There is wisdom in your own tissues.

You are your own teacher.

Negativity isn't wrong
Sadness isn't wrong
Anger isn't wrong
Envy isn't wrong
Depression isn't wrong
Anxiety isn't wrong.

When you find safety in your body, you can let each emotion feed you
Reach you
Hear you.

In the feeling
There is healing.

Self-help profits off of our self-doubt
The only help you need is in remembering your wholeness
Enoughness
Connection to all beings

Remember.

The more I trust the timing of my life
I know that what is mine is on its way
The more I delve into the inevitable mystery of being a human
I create an intimacy
An opening
A doorway
With this moment
Now.

Don't look to others for the answers that you so desperately seek; turn that seeking into being and allow your whole body to savour the wisdom that is available when you get quiet.

How often have I unleashed a hurricane
Expecting someone else to hold it
Be with it
Breathe with it
Tell me everything will be okay

How often have I outsourced my anchor
My centre
Expecting someone else to tether me back to earth
Back to belonging
Back to safety

Oh, safety
How often have I expected someone else to make me feel safe
As if to say
Baby, it's okay to be yourself
You're not alone
All of you is welcome

It's a dance, you see
We have to be able to hold ourselves, by ourselves
And
We need others to to help us heal

We are mammals who thrive in connection
Primal in nature
Of this earth, interdependent
We rely on each other and yet
We each need to find our centre

Even in chaos we can still embody
The rock in which our waves can crash against
The anchor that keeps us in place amidst the storm
The riverbanks that show us where and how to flow
The trees who sway knowing that despite the threatening wind
We are still tethered
We are still rooted
We grow deeper to stand tall

No one can do our healing for us
That's our job
Yet we cannot heal alone

Can you feel this nuance
Can you be with both?

Sometimes we have to hurt people
If we are being honest with ourselves
It's more important to me to burn some bridges
Than please and appease
Keeping the peace
While my insides
Light on fire.

Forgive for you
And for you alone
Holding onto your fire
Curses poison in your veins
Get angry
Stomp your feet
Howl at the moon
And then be free.

I realize now
When I let go a little
And then a little more
My world doesn't crumble
Nor does anything fall apart but the tension in my shoulders
My spine
The space between my eyebrows and I begin to understand
Embody
The calm depths of the ocean
Glass-like and without a ripple yet a steady undercurrent
Boastings its power when its chaos becomes rhythmic
When its rigidity becomes as smooth as the sea.

[let go]

The only way to experience water is to immerse in it
You cannot grab it
You cannot reach it
You cannot hold it

Be soft

What happens
When you let yourself float?

No effort
No strain
Breath by breath

What happens
When you let yourself be held?

We're often threatened by the artist's mind. She doesn't think like the rest of the world does. So we put her in a container because surely that's what she needs: containment. It's a great idea until the container gets too small. It's always too small. She begins reaching, trying to find her edges. Once her fingers touch the walls and she knows where she is again she begins to push -- gently at first and then with a little more force; she must break free. She wants to know what's on the other side. She needs to know. No matter where she is, no matter who or what cages her, she will always rid herself of her constraints. She is edgeless. Bottom-less. Always liquid in state.

When she is water, she is free.

My body that used to be made of earth is now water
Fluid in mind and in stature
When habit forces me to grip tighter
When I feel control rear its head again
When I start to panic and want to dry my well
Starve myself of the thirst that was finally quenched
Steal myself of the weight of my womb and the grounding I feel in
my hips
I place both hands on my belly
Feel her rise and feel her fall
Rise and fall
Until my water is once again still
Until I am reminded of home.

I paint in watercolour and am reminded
of how little
I have control

One colour merges into the next
But I resist interfering;

Slower

The green bleeds into blue
Turning into something between the two
It flows past the line I drew in pencil but stops at a new place
Always the right place
The purple is no longer purple but something warmer
One line here
One there
The piece breathes a life of its own
Somehow every movement
Perfectly imperfect
No control yet
Led by an intelligence of its own.

"You're fine."

This phrase escaped my mouth before my brain was aware of it. I was doing a somatic therapy session and my therapist asked my body to tell me what it felt -- no, what it knew -- deep in its core.

"You're fine," my body told me.

We continued. I was lying on the ground and tracking where my body met the earth. My calves, hips, upper back, and head made contact with the soft floor beneath me. Without control or instigation, my body was breathing itself. I could feel these big, expansive breaths filling me up from my toes to the top of my head. On each exhale, I went deeper. The place between my eyebrows released and I let go of any sense of holding. My bellybutton wasn't tucked into my spine as I'd been taught in yoga but was instead soft, fluid, and watery. Like a child's belly, I thought.

She began to activate my nervous system, and asked me to think of a challenging time in my life -- something that had happened more recently. She asked me what I noticed happening to my body.

"Well," I said, as I tracked the happenings that I seemed to have no control of, "my head is moving forward and my chest is collapsing. Pain is in my belly and it's like I'm closing in on myself -- like I'm freezing."

"Now," she said, "we're going to follow this through. We're going to let your body do exactly what it wants. I'll be here."

So I let go of anticipating and let my body lead the way. And lead, it did. I curled up into a little ball and tears were streaming down my cheeks. I was shaking, trembling. I felt her hands cup the back of my neck.

"You've made it though," she said. "And for every hurt you experience, you always make it through. Now come back."

My body began to open and soon I was lying on my back again. I felt sensation behind my eyes, signalling another headache. But this time the pain travelled upwards and things became still again. Even. Empty -- a good kind of empty.

"What would your body tell you now?" She asked.

"You're still fine," I said.

And I wept again, not out of pain but because of how innately wise we are when we can get quiet enough to listen.

Be in the unclear
The mud
The stuck
The yuck
The place you don't want to be
That you're not sure about
That you're tempted to run away from
Pause long enough to ask yourself:
What is here for me
Despite it all?

"As it is," she told me.

As it is.

When life feels uncomfortable
When it's not what you want
When it's too much
When it's confusing
When it's hard
For a moment longer
Let it be *as it is.*

The more we can feel the tough stuff
The more we can feel the joy
These are two sides of the same coin
Make room for both.

Your soul has woven a web of a thousand stories. You come from your own lineage of dreams and maybe you can hear them speak to you if you become available. If you dive into your waters and see what's beneath the surface.

You are the same as the plants, the trees, the soils, the bees, the tides.

What happens when you make space to *listen?*

You know when you get what you want
And you second guess it
"Is this right?"
"Is this for me?"
"Am I worthy of this?"
If it wasn't supposed to happen
It wouldn't be happening
Please trust
Every
Single
Intuitive
Piece
Of
You.

I run through the woods
Up the muddy trail and to the vista
I pause at the top
Heart racing and lungs open in aliveness
Trees protecting me and a lake in front
Wide open, it's as if
She's waiting for me to place my wishes
I kneel to the earth and
A sigh escapes my lips
As if I forgot.

Life is fluid when I don't know what I want
Really, though
Do we ever know what we want?
Trained to be ambitious
It's a rebellion to drop in
Right here
This breath
Not needing anything to be different
While knowing that nothing stays the same.

When you remove the 't' in 'there'
You arrive 'here'
Maybe we should only spell out
What's right in front of us.

I want the quiet to be a little more quiet
The space to be a little more spacious
I want life to feel like it does when I'm on the road
When curiosity leads my heart forwards
Onwards
I want to remember
That home is not so much a place but rather a feeling embodied by
The wildflowers in the meadow I pass
The rugged forest of this island's coastline
The sand that massages my toes
The deer that treads lightly ahead
The river flowing through craggy rocks
Gnarly roots, exposed
Alpine creek, thirsty
The distant, hungry howls at a bright moon
The catch of the salmon by the black bear's able claws
The always changing, cyclical tides
A remembrance that has me knowing that all of nature is mirrored
in me
What's out there is in here
Her abundance
Her volatility
Her moody skies
Her vibrant shades
Her generous givings
Her thunderous musings
Her soft places to land
So let's remember
Let's get closer
Let's embody our home
With compassionate
Committed
Awakening curiosity.

I live on the earthly realm but I commune with Spirit
She is not separate from me, though
I am Her.
She shows up in the way my pen moves; the way these words write
themselves
She is the flowers that bloom and the leaves that shed
She is weather patterns
Fertile soil
Stormy seas
The moon-lit sky
But I can too easily forget Her
When I have tunnel vision and life feels like a series of tasks
I miss the subtleties of this wisdom
The signs she sends me get missed amongst the to-do's
The call to just be gets skewed with the habit to go
And the moment I submit to stillness
The point I ease into rest
She finally has space to speak up
Sometimes in poetry, but it can be more discreet;
The lotus flower that once again begins to open again
The dandelion making its way through the cracks in my porch
My water-stained pages reminding me it's okay to go there
To fully go there.

And during my day, when She feels safe enough
She asks me to remember:

"Trust, trust, trust your inner wisdom."

You will not step in the same stream twice
The water that rushes over your feet continues to
Move
Change
Bleed
Can you let the steady chaos
The ever-moving current
Teach you something
About impermanence?

Taught to distrust our innate wisdom, our womb pipes up from time to time. Her voice getting louder as She asks us, "When will you listen to my intelligence again?"

Her brilliance is in the way she can change
She is fluid because she knows that
Even when she spits embers from her tongue she is mostly water

She flows with ease over the jagged rocks along the ocean floor;
She remembers how stillness always comes after the storm

She knows she will never understand all of life's mysteries so she
surrenders
Again and again
She surrenders.

I go to the forest with a basket of petals
As I walk I place them on her floor
One here, one there
At her roots, near the yarrow, next to the dandelions
A small feat, but an intentional one
A few more steps ahead I stop at her trunk
I look up
Branches outstretched like an umbrella
Protecting me from the elements because she knows how to
weather the storm but I do not
Steady, only when I see her as my teacher do I understand her
strength
She grows deeper to stand tall
No rigidity, she lets herself sway
The wind takes her leaves but she remains in her centre
Reaching, she finds support from her
Neighbours
Elders
Ancestors
In community, her innate intelligence does its work
And as I walk through her maze
I gaze in awe at her diverse system
The spirit in all beings
And I place petals on her floor.

I am a student of life
The wilderness my classroom
Relationships my teachers
I will never climb the corporate ladder but I promise I will learn
just the same
A simple day to day
Hours filled with ease
I don't need the grandiose
To be happy.

We will never leave behind our inner wild
Nor our animalistic instincts
Instead, let's remember.

[come home to you]

Restless wanderer
Your head has been in the clouds for a long time
Everything you want is over there,
Or so you think.

Restless wanderer
You've been avoiding getting quiet because it's as if you know
That the more empty your mind gets
The more you can hear.

Restless wanderer
I know you don't want to listen to what I have to say but
It seems that you think
You have to go far
Do big things
And prove yourself over and over.

Restless wanderer
Do you know that who you are is enough?
Do you know that what you want is okay?
Do you know that everything is here for you?

Everything is here for you,
I come through you when you write these words on the pages of
your journal
It's not embodied yet but I'm waiting for you to remember
That what you think you want has been conditioned
That what you really need is waiting patiently
In the soils, the moss, the earth
Lower
Deeper
Here.

Restless wanderer
What if the suffering you feel
Is not a problem to be solved but rather
A healthy response
To an unhealthy world?

Roots take time to grow
And flowers can only bloom when they feel safe
When they feel ready.

Restless wanderer
What if blooming
Just felt a little different this season?

Your heart is bold and brazen
Etched with scars of your experience
An emblem of time blanketed in silk
Powerfully soft
Backbone of steel
You don't question your inner world
You listen to her inquiry.

Sometimes I feel like I'm in the middle of the ocean
Unsure where the land is and I don't know which direction to
swim
So everyday I go to the sea to remind myself that being
amidst its unpredictability isn't so scary
I submerge myself in her waters
My limbs sway under the surface like seaweed
My hair wild like the tentacles of the jellyfish
I cry my tears of grief for the old world until I remember that
my tears are just like the sea's

Everyday I go into the ocean
Alive with her rage and dis-ease
I float to remember that nothing is lost here
That in this unknown joy can co-exist with chaos
That it's not one or the other
That in this place between the old and the new is still a place
It's not stagnant
It's not wrong
It's here

Patience.

The access point to the magic we can co-create is the sea of
in-betweens
Can you meet yourself?

Did you catch that?
Repeat after me:
Joy can coexist with chaos.

Your compass is not in the mechanical tool tied to your map
It's in the quickening of your own pulse
The words that wait to be spoken in your throat
The gravitational pull to people
The surefire telling of which direction to follow
Which person to turn towards and rest your head upon as the sky
gets dark
And the moon rises, proudly.

You're sick, they said
Here are some pills, they said
Your ups and downs aren't normal
Your cyclical nature is wrong
Your intuition is off-kilter
You are separate.

You're not safe, but these pills are
10mg in the morning, they said
Your good days won't be so good
But your bad days won't be so bad
You wanted steadiness, right?

The buzz made me feel like
I could take on anything
Like there was nothing I couldn't achieve
That I could do more
Push more
Strive more, but

When pain is stolen, so is joy

After a while, it went away --
Take 20mg now, they said
But something felt off;
I realized I was trying to contain myself
Be more palatable
Not for me
But for them.

Why were my feelings so scary in the first place?

I weaned myself off
Let every repressed part of me bubble to the surface
Ideas spilled out onto the pages of my journal
My pen scribbled poems, words, doodles
I felt different
Vibrant
Creative
I found my medicine.

I became unwilling to see some parts of me as wrong
I became unwilling to compartmentalize my wholeness.

I wasn't sick
I wasn't broken
I hadn't yet questioned the system that placed me in this category
I had only questioned myself.

Everything I feel shouts my aliveness to the world
My rhythm aligns with the Earth's -- I can hear her
The moon that controls the tides also waxes and wanes within me.

Slowly, I'm becoming less afraid of these feelings
Feelings that used to sweep into my life like a hurricane
I've found my own internal shoreline
I've found the rocks that catch my waves
I've found safety in creation.

My feelings created this book
My feelings are sacred
They remind me
I am alive.

The answers to the questions I seek
The wisdom that has been passed down through my lineage
Is in my tissues
my bones

It lays there dormant;
I am trained to look outside of myself for
validation
confirmation
truth

In moments of remembrance
I understand that I can give myself what I seek

I don't need answers from boyfriends
girlfriends
strangers
gurus

Underneath the noise and the 'not enough' narratives that run rampant
I can give myself what I need
crave
desire

Beneath it all
In that quiet
In that mystery
Here I am
Here I am
Here I am.

Freedom seeking
In a time when we are strangled by invisible cages
Caught in the trap of
Keeping up
Keeping going
I wonder what would happen
If we could shed our conditioning
Live for joy
Rooted in earth and swimming in water
If pleasure could be a revolution.

Our bodies are vessels for pleasure. And our pleasure is the most rebellious thing in the world. Taught to strive, produce, and achieve, pleasure is a loosening. A relaxing. A dropping in -- right here -- and seeing the good that's here for us in our every cell.

Feel that.

Everything worthwhile happens in connection with the here and now
So please
Go slower.

Pleasure is synonymous with creativity.

Nothing worthwhile is over there
It's all here for you
It's in the edgeless
Bottomless
Never-ending
Liquid state.

I give up wondering when my life will finally start and
instead get curious
About the thousands of cycles
Endings and beginnings
Deaths and rebirths
Inhales and exhales
Changing seasons
In-betweens
Here.

If only I could have seen that all of these years chasing everything outside of myself would lead me back to where I started: Already whole, already complete, and already enough.

When you let the flow carry you, it does so in a way that you can't predict
When you let the flow carry you, you remember Her intelligence

Keep going
Keep remembering
Let yourself be liquid.

Don't you think it's time you start listening to your soul?

She's always speaking to you and through you, but not through your mental chatter or ceaseless thoughts.

She's the voice that's behind the noise. The voice you hear when your head is clear; when you're creating and flowing and receiving what life is giving you.

She's the voice you hear that spurs you into action; that all-knowing kind of action. That 'this is exactly what is supposed to happen right now' kind of action. The voice you hear when you are safe.

She's soft but carries power. And every time you ignore her, she gets a bit quieter. She doesn't understand why you try to muscle your way through life, or attempt to bypass your body.

She doesn't understand.

But every time you listen, you give her a little more weight. She gets a little taller, rises a little higher, becomes a little stronger. She starts to trust herself, too.

See for yourself how when you listen to her she never leads you astray.

People pleasing is no longer my job
Nor is walking on eggshells
I give up when it's time
I press onwards when I need to
And when I blow things up I send a prayer before
I sort through the rubble
Looking for gold.

These walls you've tried so hard to keep up
To stay safe
Are asking to come down

Who are you
When your boundaries are not so much earth
But water?

Who are you
When you let yourself be soft?

I don't know where to go
I simply just follow my flow
Plans change at every turn
Open to chances to grow, love, and learn
I find myself in unexpected places
Leaving parts of my heart as my only traces
Wishing I had more direction
But knowing control is the mind's false protection
Letting go of where I thought life would lead me
Surrendering to the divine and synchronicity
I don't need to know where to go
I simply just follow my flow

[written on a two-day train from kerala to punjab, india]

They say that when you want to release something
Go to the river
When you want to take pause
Go to the ocean
And when you want to create anew
Go to the lake

So immerse yourself in water
Ask Her for what you need
Let yourself be guided.

There's a hidden network here. Something happening underground -- quiet enough to bypass it but loud enough that you can't help but pay attention. It's a whispering revolution; wisdom uprising. The feminine who will no longer be repressed; the feminine who remembers that nature is inside of her.

Together, we stand. But what's our vision? Not yours, not mine, but ours? It's confronting to shift from the individual to the whole and we are beginning to feel this. We can no longer shy away from it -- this inkling that seems to vibrate from our toes to our hearts when our feet are planted in the soil. The looming sense of change.

How much do we value our home? We are visitors -- here for a short time before we gift this place to our kids and their kids and their kids. How do we want to leave it? Can we do more good than harm?

How do we spend our time in celebration and reverence to our interconnectedness? In community, hand in hand, free of the devices that distract us from our innate desire -- and need -- for connection.

Where did our wisdom go? We are lost in the belief that we are the species that only wins once we dominate.

We have strayed so far.

We can no longer dominate.
We can no longer push onwards like we always have.
We are no longer winning.

Pause long enough to feel it -- that pulse of the Earth that is communicating with you. She is asking for help. She needs our voices. She's calling the stewards, the rebels, the healers, the do-ers.

She's calling you.

Hear her. Feel her. It's okay to be with her pain. Keep your heart open to all of it.

She's calling you.

What now?

On some level we do not feel safe
We see the trees that stand next to the clearcut;
Trees that take in our toxicity without question and provide us
the air we breathe
Trees that are an extension of us

We do not feel safe yet we resist turning towards pain
We go back to our individual pursuits in frantic speed
We're on a quest!
Survival of the fittest!
Climb the ladder!
Top of the food chain!
Get there -- quicker!
Forge ahead!
Move out of the way!

We play the game of winning at the system because we don't
know another way
Even though there is some part of us
Some inkling and nudging and persistent thumping deep inside
of us that asks us to look closer
Get lower
Go slower
Take our rose-coloured glasses off and see that there is a new
way
A way that is not paved but a way all the same
It's prickly and requires bushwhacking
It's the scenic route;
The route that climbs up the mountain
Treading in a spiral

Stopping at the river to splash our faces open with wonder
It's rebellious and foreign
It's willing and asking
It's the path of resistance
Of inconvenience
Of inefficiency
Of wide open, heart-centred space
Where Mother Earth comes first
Not before us, but as part of us.

Can you feel her?

I walk on the trail feeling pain rise from the soles of my feet to my hips and back down again
The line of my ancestors is not just my elders but the trees
They need us because they are us
The wisdom keepers left are the old growth
But even then, there are hardly any left
Few and far between
Whispering for change is no longer working
We must stand up
Be loud
Tall
Proud
Bold
Because without the tree spirit
We are lost.

What happens when I ask my body
About what she wants
Is that she tells me she wants more
More play
More pleasure
More connection
More earth
More birth
More.

And she also wants less
She tells me that resting is okay
And so is trusting
And so is not knowing
And so is allowing
And so is loosening the grip of control.

She tells me to soften and
Honour desire
Yes yes yes
This is what she wants most
To let myself yearn for so much more and so much less
A continual paradox that can only be navigated by feeling.

Desire;
There is no roadmap to get there
Her way is not linear
But she knows the next step
And the next
And the next
And the next
As if every time she surrenders
Her heart cracks open
Just a little bit wider.

It's all here for you --
Every little thing you desire.

I wake up with hope in my chest
An open throat that can speak what I need
Because I no longer shove what I want under the rug
I tell you so you can hold my words in your palms
And meet me here.

She's soft
And underneath her pillowy surface is a little fire
A little earth
Some air, even
Just by being her we yearn for her
We want more of her when she remembers the waters in her hips
The slowness in her hands
The fervour in her speech; a strong spine that embodies what she is
here for
Because when she's at home in her cells she is the edge of the
flame and the dewy moonlit hue of the morning tide.

She is that powerful.
You are that powerful.

Do you remember?

This body of mine,
She carries me up mountains
Submerges into the sea
Grounds her feet into the earth so she can rise higher.

This body of mine,
She speaks what's on her heart and
Discerns when it's safe to open
She tells me when she needs more
Time
Rest
Patience
Pleasure
Receptivity.

Wise like her ancestors and their ancestors
She carries the knowledge that's been passed down her lineage
She is being, embodied
An overflowing cup of enoughness yet
How quick I am to scorn her
To ask her shape to be something different
To get caught in thinking she needs to exert when she just wants to be.

She just wants to be.

This body of mine,
She's adjusted to structure but is tired of being contained
She craves the freedom of pushing her own boundaries
Seeing what's beneath her surface so she can
Feel herself more deeply.

And when I give her permission to accept her nature as cyclical
As winding
As movement
As constant change
I come home to myself
As if this body of mine has waited to say:

Finally,
Here you are.
Here I am.

See what happens when you remember that you are all of nature inside.

Maybe that's where the love is -- when we can have so much compassion that we finally begin giving it to ourselves. When we can walk alone and trust that those who are meant to will join us in our march. When our faith is so strong that we refuse to settle for less -- we know that what's ours is on its way. We know this deep in our core, our bones, our blood.

We know this.

I think I've been alone when I forget that I'm part of the interconnected whole
The systems that weave above and below me
Within me
In my muscles
In my bones.

It's too easy to forget that we are part of something greater
As far as the cosmos reach the edgeless universe
We are together.

When you realize that life has no end goal -- that your entire human experience is simply a process of becoming -- you can meet each stage of your journey with an inner knowing that you're exactly where you need to be.

Your mind, body and spirit want to work as a team. But they can only do so when you honour your process. When you meet yourself where you're at, and say, "hey, I trust you."

Let your experience of becoming take up your entire life -- with less rushing, doubting, questioning, and wondering where you're going.

You're simply going.

I am at once the oldest I've ever been and also the youngest. Despite my body which tells me I am a woman, my heart slowly returns to a time that I was led by my soul's desires. It returns to my young self, my child self. I vow to stay here, to come back here, to always remind myself of home.

Go into other dimensions. Rise into the clouds. Visit your past lives. Tune into source.

But please, don't forget to care for your body. Nurture your skin, find daily movement, cry when you need to, laugh from your belly, eat from the earth.

Your body is what houses your soul. When you're in connection with what she needs, you become more connected and intimate with all parts of your aliveness.

Do not bypass your human body in thinking that there is something greater than you. That something greater is you.

Maybe the scariest part is realizing that I was whole all along
That my only job was to relish in my fullness
Without thinking there was something wrong
Or missing.

For a long time, there was resistance to being in my body.
It was scary.
It's still scary.
Bypassing my body -- transcending upwards -- is so much easier.
When I'm in my body, there's no escaping: she knows exactly what she wants.
There's nowhere to hide.
There's nowhere to run.
Presence.

When I don't listen, she loses trust. Her cues become confusing -- or they're missed all together. Intuition gets muddied -- she can't feel it as strongly. The 'yes' and 'no' she receives becomes one and the same.

This makes her angry. Her voice is firm, and what she wants most is to be listened to. So slowly, I'm becoming more available to her. Making space for her. Hearing her. I've started to ask her what she wants. And even though she wants to scream, she takes a breath before she speaks. Softly, yet with fire at the edges of her words, this is what she tells me:

I want to lay on the earth.
I want to feel the soil beneath me, as well as the moss. I want to feel its cool dampness without needing it to be different, but rather relish in the discomfort it brings and let it remind me that I am part of its aliveness. An aliveness that is all encompassing.

I want to be guided by all five senses first, spirit second.
I want to laugh at the conditioning that tells me to do more to be a better version of myself. I want to choose being instead
A little longer in bed
Abundance in everything.

Abundance that comes from my root, not from my third eye
Abundance that is grounded in the now, not the not yet
Abundance that comes from my desires that lead my way.

Desires; I'll let those be my compass. Because I don't want to be
scared of desiring anymore.

I want to indulge in the simple pleasures. Not the grandiose or the
adrenaline-fueled, but that first sip of coffee. Afternoon nap. Rain on
my face. Brushed hair. Salty breeze. Sun-kissed glow. No makeup.
Homemade cooking. Cozy blanket. Clean sheets. Dirty feet. Tired body.
Warm water. Natural beauty.

I want to go back to the earth, back to my essence, back to where
everything once started and play here. Barefoot, play here.

So please, start lower
Go slower.

I want to come back to the earth again
Feel her pulse
And equally her grief and rage.
I want to rest here
Nest here
Stop running away from here.

I want to listen to her intensity and wait for her to nudge me to what's
next. No more bypassing. Life from my root, not my third eye; it all
starts lower.

Lower, lower, lower.

I want to fill every one of my needs so that I can meet the world as a whole person. So I can share from an overflowing cup. So I can attract souls that meet and revel in my wholeness rather than my wounds.

I want to float in water and let myself be held. I want to feel music fill up every cell as it dances in my veins. I want to taste every morsel of my food. I want space -- space to create and space to just be.

Lower, lower, lower.

No more bypassing
No more running
No more escaping what's here
It's time to be brave
It's time to stay
So go lower
Just a little bit lower
I promise, it's soft down here
Join me down here.
Lower, lower, lower.
Come home to me.

[gratitude]

Mama
for being all that you are.

Elyse Turpin
for being the first eyes on my work, listening to my doubts, and helping
me dig deep to share this collection.

Kyla Zeniuk
for being the best space holder, taking in this work in with so much
care, and helping me make the final touches.

Sophie Josephina
for helping me to reconnect with my feminine nature and wisdom,
reminding me of my essence, helping me feel at home in myself.

Megan Field
For reminding me of my relationship with nature, and the role it plays
in my life + healing.

Jacquline Gautier
for reminding me of my connection to water, for helping me remember
my power.

Penny Maday Ciochetti
for connecting me to my childlike self that loved to play and make art.

My family
for giving me two seasons in a cabin by the sea to rest and remember.
For those on the other side, thank you for connecting to me and through
me. You helped this book be born.

All words and artwork created by Riley Webster.

[author]

Riley Webster is a storyteller, creative, and
other evolving titles living on Vancouver
Island, British Columbia.

When she's not creating, she enjoys cooking,
playing outside with her dog, movement of all
kinds, and spending time with the people she
loves.

Connect with her on Instagram:
@byrileywebster
Visit her website: www.byrileywebster.ca

CPSIA information can be obtained
at www.ICGtesting.com
Printed in the USA
BVHW021138141121
621606BV00012B/95

9 780228 862499